THE INCREDIBLE JOURNEY TO THE CENTRE OF THE ATOM

> *I am about to embark on a journey. But it is a journey like no other. Not simply a trip from place to place of the sort people make every day. This is a voyage from everything to almost nothing. From the unimaginably big to the incredibly small. From the Universe (which may be 100 million billion billion billion billion kilometres wide) to the particles which make up a single atom (perhaps smaller than one tenth of a billion billionth of a millimetre across). As I travel from one to the other, different scenes come into focus. I will try to describe for you what I experience...*

UNIVERSE

"*IT IS EXTREMELY COLD, absolutely silent and very dark. Way off in the distance are splashes of light. They look like distant snowflakes caught in the beam of a torch. I speed towards one, and as I do I can see that it is made up of hundreds of smaller lights packed together. On I travel for what seems like an eternity, aiming for one of those smaller lights. It, too, now seems to consist of a cluster of lights. Thirty or so, I think, scattered hither and thither. But the lights are different shapes: some misty spheres, some blobs, some spiral whirlpools. Fascinated, I zoom in towards one of those twinkling spirals, and am soon rewarded by a glorious sight...*"

THE UNIVERSE MAY CONTAIN ABOUT 100 BILLION GALAXIES • THE UNIVERSE WAS MORE THAN 10,000 MILLION DEGREES CELSIUS

SECOND AFTER THE BIG BANG, THE TEMPERATURE OF THE UNIVERSE

POSSIBLE FATE OF THE UNIVERSE (I)

The Universe will keep on expanding forever

UNIVERSE

THE UNIVERSE is everything we know – and much more besides. The vast stretches of outer space, planets, moons, everything around you (and including yourself) are all part of the Universe.

Distances in the Universe are so vast we have to use a special measure to record them: the *light-year*, or the distance that light travels in one year (about 9,460,000,000,000 kilometres). The most distant objects we know in the Universe are calculated to be more than 13 billion light-years away!

Most of the Universe looks like empty space, but scattered across it are billions of GALAXIES. These are enormous collections of stars, gas and dust. They come in different shapes and sizes: some are giant spheres, others magnificent spirals, still others irregular blobs. Galaxies are by no means evenly positioned in space: they tend to group together in clusters. For example, our own galaxy, the Milky Way, is part of a cluster of about 30 galaxies. Other clusters may contain thousands of galaxies. Clusters of galaxies, in turn, make up superclusters.

Many scientists think that the Universe was born in a colossal explosion called the Big Bang. In this explosion, about 15 billion years ago, all matter, energy, space and time were created. Such was the force of the explosion that, to this day, the Universe is still expanding. Gigantic clouds of dust and gas have clumped together over billions of years to produce galaxies, stars and planets – the Universe as we know it.

POSSIBLE FATE OF THE UNIVERSE (2)
The Universe will reach a maximum size and then contract: the "Big Crunch."

SOME LARGE GALAXIES MAY HAVE MORE THAN 1,000 BILLION STARS • A NEARBY CLUSTER OF GALAXIES, CALLED VIRGO, CONTAINS AT LEAST 2,500 GALAXIES • A FRACTION OF

THE UNIVERSE CONTAINS BILLIONS OF GALAXIES • THE UNIVERSE CONTAINS BILLIONS OF GALAXIES •

GALAXY

" *IT'S LIKE ONE ENORMOUS catherine wheel: a vast, shimmering, flat coil of stars and gas slowly turning before me. There are yellow, orange, red and blue lights gleaming amid the brilliant sea of white. At the centre there is a low bulge, pushing outwards from the spiral as if something was about to burst through. I can make out several arms uncoiling from the bulge. Clouds of stars and twinkling dust, studded with bright blue stars, swirl in the outer reaches before the arms fade away into space. After a long voyage through empty space, the marvellously detailed pattern of this island of stars is simply amazing.* "

OUR GALAXY IS ONE OF BILLIONS IN THE UNIVERSE • OUR GALAXY IS ONE OF BILLIONS IN THE UNIVERSE •

IT WOULD TAKE A FURTHER 100 BILLION YEARS TO REACH THE FAR SIDE OF OUR GALAXY BY J

IT WOULD TAKE 5 MILLION YEARS • IT WOULD TAKE 5 MILLION YEARS

PROXIMA CENTAURI, IT WOULD TAKE TO THE NEAREST STAR, PROXIMA CENTAURI, IT WOULD

YOU COULD TRAVEL BY JUMBO JET TO THE NEAREST STAR,

BLACK HOLE

Cygnus X-1: gas from a giant star is gradually being dragged into a black hole

BLACK HOLE

GALAXY

GALAXY is the place in space where stars are found – in their billions. Every star you see in the night sky is part of the Milky Way, the galaxy to which our own star, the Sun, belongs (although on a clear night, you can glimpse one or two galaxies that lie beyond the Milky Way). Like our Sun, all these stars are giant spinning balls of hot, luminous gas, but they lie very much farther away from us. Almost certainly, many will have planets that orbit around them, perhaps some where there are living things.

Our galaxy, the Milky Way, is a spiral galaxy. It is named after the misty trail of stars across the night sky – our edge-on view of the galaxy. Seen from above, the arms of the spiral radiate out from the bulging centre and contain young, bright stars. Our star, the Sun, lies on one of these spiral arms, about three-fifths of the way out from the centre of the galaxy.

Stars come in different colours – according to how old they are. Blue stars are young and hot; red stars are old and cool. Orange and yellow stars (including the Sun) are young to middle-aged and moderately hot.

Stars begin as clouds of dust and gas which collapse to form a bright, hot core. A medium-sized star, like our Sun, can glow brightly for billions of years until its hydrogen fuel is used up. A very few giant stars eventually explode (a supernova) before forming BLACK HOLES, regions of space so dense that nothing, not even light, can escape the pull of its GRAVITY. Many galaxies – including perhaps even our own Milky Way – have a black hole at their centres.

A BLACK HOLE IS INCREDIBLY DENSE – EQUIVALENT TO A MARBLE WITH A MASS THE SAME AS PLANET EARTH • THE MILKY WAY GALAXY TAKES MORE THAN 200 MILLION YEARS TO COMPLETE ONE REVOLUTION

OUR SOLAR SYSTEM LIES IN THE MILKY WAY GALAXY • OUR SOLAR SYSTEM LIES IN THE MILKY WAY GALAXY •

LIFE AND DEATH OF A STAR

1 Dense cloud of dust and gas forms 2 Dust and gas blown clear 3 Star and planets form 4 No change for millions of years 5 Star grows into red giant 6 Supernova or planetary nebula 7 Tiny, super-dense star

LIFE AND DEATH OF A STAR

SOLAR SYSTEM

" I SPEED TOWARDS a gleaming yellow star. As I go, I catch sight of different coloured balls floating in space. A small grey one, two large blue ones, then a great golden sphere encircled by shining rings: a magical sight. Looming larger still, a giant globe streaked with bands of gold, white, yellow and scarlet spins slowly. A block of ice hurtles past me also heading for the star. A long, brilliant white tail like a streak of icy mist stretches in its wake. Then, rocks everywhere. Some big lumps, others tiny specks whistling close by. I dodge through them. A small, brick-red globe comes into view, then one mostly blue but with streaks of white. Two more balls lie closer to the star, but I approach instead this strangely alluring blue-and-white sphere... "

MORE THAN ONE MILLION EARTHS COULD FIT INSIDE THE SUN

PLUTO IS LARGER THAN BOTH MERCURY AND PLUTO

JUPITER'S 16 MOONS

THE LARGEST OF JUPITER

THE SUN IS A BALL OF EXTREMELY HOT GAS

Arches of glowing gas rise from the surface

Jupiter and Earth are shown to scale

THE SUN IS A BALL OF EXTREMELY HOT GAS

THE SUN IS ONE OF BILLIONS OF STARS IN THE MILKY WAY

IS MILLION °C AT ITS CENTRE

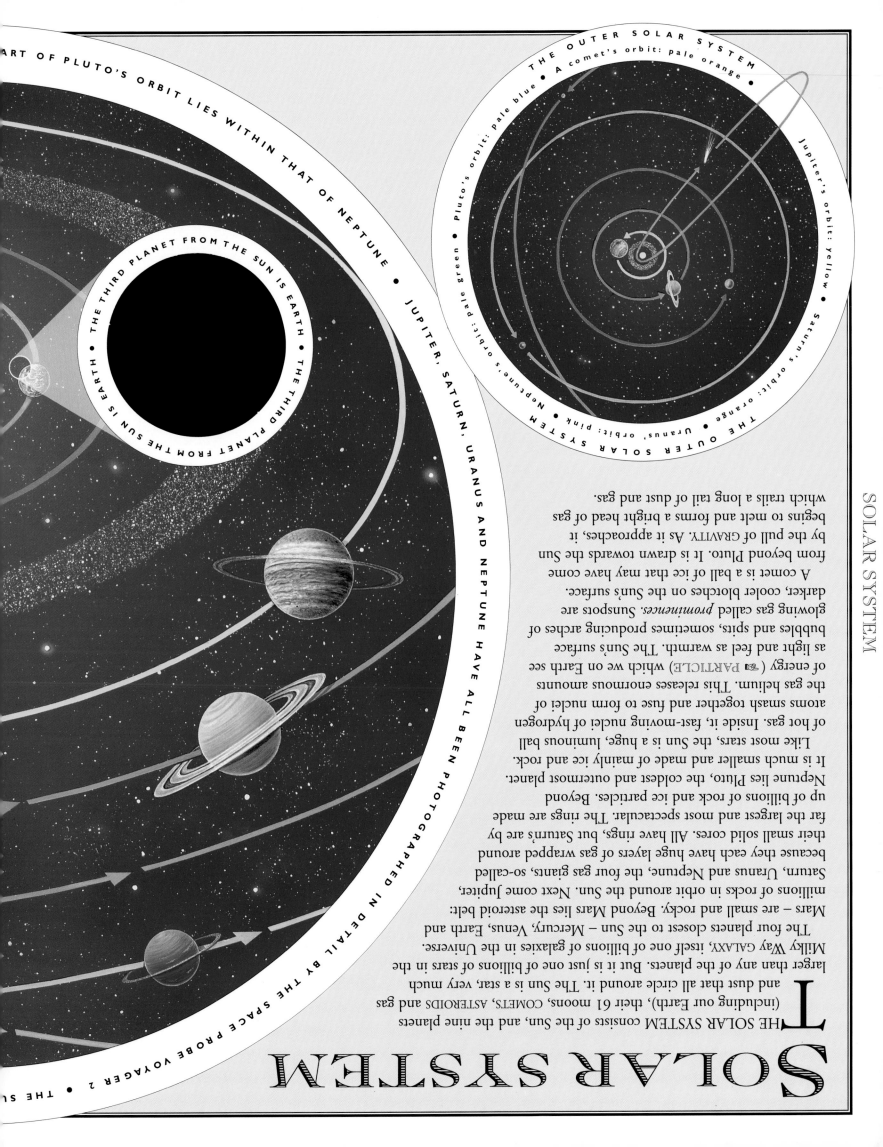

SOLAR SYSTEM

THE SOLAR SYSTEM consists of the Sun, and the nine planets (including our Earth), their 61 moons, COMETS, ASTEROIDS and gas and dust that all circle around it. The Sun is a star, very much larger than any of the planets. But it is just one of billions of stars in the Milky Way GALAXY, itself one of billions of galaxies in the Universe.

The four planets closest to the Sun — Mercury, Venus, Earth and Mars — are small and rocky. Beyond Mars lies the asteroid belt: millions of rocks in orbit around the Sun. Next come Jupiter, Saturn, Uranus and Neptune, the four gas giants, so-called because they each have huge layers of gas wrapped around their small solid cores. All have rings, but Saturn's are by far the largest and most spectacular. The rings are made up of billions of rock and ice particles. Beyond Neptune lies Pluto, the coldest and outermost planet. It is much smaller and made of mainly ice and rock.

Like most stars, the Sun is a huge, luminous ball of hot gas. Inside it, fast-moving nuclei of hydrogen atoms smash together and fuse to form nuclei of the gas helium. This releases enormous amounts of energy (☞ PARTICLE) which we on Earth see as light and feel as warmth. The Sun's surface bubbles and spits, sometimes producing arches of glowing gas called *prominences*. Sunspots are darker, cooler blotches on the Sun's surface.

A comet is a ball of ice that may have come from beyond Pluto. It is drawn towards the Sun by the pull of GRAVITY. As it approaches, it begins to melt and forms a bright head of gas which trails a long tail of dust and gas.

THE OUTER SOLAR SYSTEM • A comet's orbit: pale orange • Pluto's orbit: pale blue • Jupiter's orbit: yellow • Saturn's orbit: orange • Uranus' orbit: pink • Neptune's orbit: pale green • THE OUTER SOLAR SYSTEM

PART OF PLUTO'S ORBIT LIES WITHIN THAT OF NEPTUNE • JUPITER, SATURN, URANUS AND NEPTUNE HAVE ALL BEEN PHOTOGRAPHED IN DETAIL BY THE SPACE PROBE VOYAGER 2 • THE SUN

THE THIRD PLANET FROM THE SUN IS EARTH • THE THIRD PLANET FROM THE SUN IS EARTH

EARTH

A BEAUTIFUL, BRIGHT BALL floats before me, revolving slowly. It looks like a giant marble: mostly deep blue, with wonderful, great swirling patterns of white. As I get nearer I can make out detailed shapes on the surface, and different colours, too: browns, yellows and greens. Both the top and bottom of the ball are capped by large white patches. Not too far away I can see another, smaller ball. But this one is quite different. No blues, greens or yellows at all – just a dull brown-grey surface pockmarked with craters. As I fall towards the great blue ball, for the first time I sense my movement is being slowed. And I can feel warmth.

THE TEMPERATURE AT THE EARTH'S CORE IS THOUGHT TO BE ABOUT 5000° C

THE EARTH IS ONE PLANET IN THE SOLAR SYSTEM

SLIGHTLY AT THE EQUATOR • • IT BULGES • THE EARTH IS NOT A PERFECT SPHERE: IT BULGES • EARTH

INSIDE THE EARTH

Plates moving apart ▶

Mantle

Mid-ocean ridge

Inner core

Outer core

Convection currents

Mantle

Volcano

Plates are moved by convection currents, heat rising and falling in the mantle

◀ One plate sliding beneath another

INSIDE THE EARTH

EARTH

EARTH IS THE THIRD nearest planet to the Sun. Of the nine planets, it is the only one which supports life. Because of its position relative to the Sun, it is neither too hot nor too cold for the existence of liquid water, essential to life.

The Earth's ATMOSPHERE consists mostly of nitrogen and oxygen, with some carbon dioxide and water vapour. It is thin enough to let through sunlight but thick enough to block most of the harmful RADIATION such as ultraviolet light. The atmosphere also acts like a blanket, keeping the planet at an almost even temperature, and it provides the air that animals breathe.

The Moon, by contrast, lacks both an atmosphere and water. Consequently its surface temperature is always extremely cold and there is no life.

Inside, the Earth is made up of several layers. At the centre is the core, a hot ball of iron surrounded by liquid metal. Around the core lies the MANTLE, a thick, mostly solid layer.

The Earth's crust, its rigid surface layer, is made of several slabs, called TECTONIC PLATES which fit together like the pieces of a jigsaw puzzle. The plates float on top of the mantle and are always on the move, powered by CONVECTION CURRENTS (heat circulating through the mantle). Where the plates collide or rub together they cause earthquakes and fold the crust into mountains. Where they move apart or slip under one another, molten rock (magma) from the mantle rises to the surface through volcanoes.

THE SAME SIDE OF THE MOON ALWAYS FACES TH[E]

OCEANS AND CONTINENTS MAKE UP THE EARTH'S SURFACE • OCEANS AND CONTINENTS MAKE UP THE EARTH'S SURFACE

LIGHT LEAVING THE SUN TAKES OVER EIGHT MINUTES TO REACH THE EARTH

THE EARTH TAKES 365.26 DAYS TO ORBIT THE SUN

THE EARTH'S CRUST IS DIVIDED INTO GREAT PLATES
Plate boundaries shown in red

LAND

"*RISING UP from the sea, the land forms giant, irregular shapes in different hues of brown and green. Where there are mountains, it looks like a rumpled-up blanket; deep shadows lie in the valleys, while white daubs of snow and ice lie atop the peaks. The rivers are like long, spindly, dark lines clawing their way across the surface. Many of them link up like twigs on a branch before meeting the sea. There are also wide, flat areas of land where the colours are mostly greens and yellows. I can just make out the regular criss-cross patterns of the fields and the long, straight lines of the roads. The towns look like splashes of grey. Suddenly, just below me, an aeroplane roars past, sunlight glinting on its shiny surface.*"

THE VOLCANIC ERUPTION AT KRAKATOA IN INDONESIA IN 1883 PRODUCED GIANT OCEAN WAVES WHICH TRAVELLED HALFWAY ROUND THE WORLD

OCEANS AND CONTINENTS MAKE UP THE EARTH'S SURFACE • OCEANS AND CONTINENTS MAKE UP THE EARTH'S SURFACE • OCEANS AND CONTINENTS MAKE UP THE EARTH'S SURFACE

THE AMAZON RIVER CARRIES ONE-FIFTH OF ALL THE WORLD'S FRESH WATER •

THE WATER CYCLE

Water evaporates from the sea (and land)

Clouds, masses of condensed water vapour, form

Water droplets in clouds fall as rain (or snow)

Water runs off the land into lakes and rivers

The rivers empty their water into the sea

THE WATER CYCLE

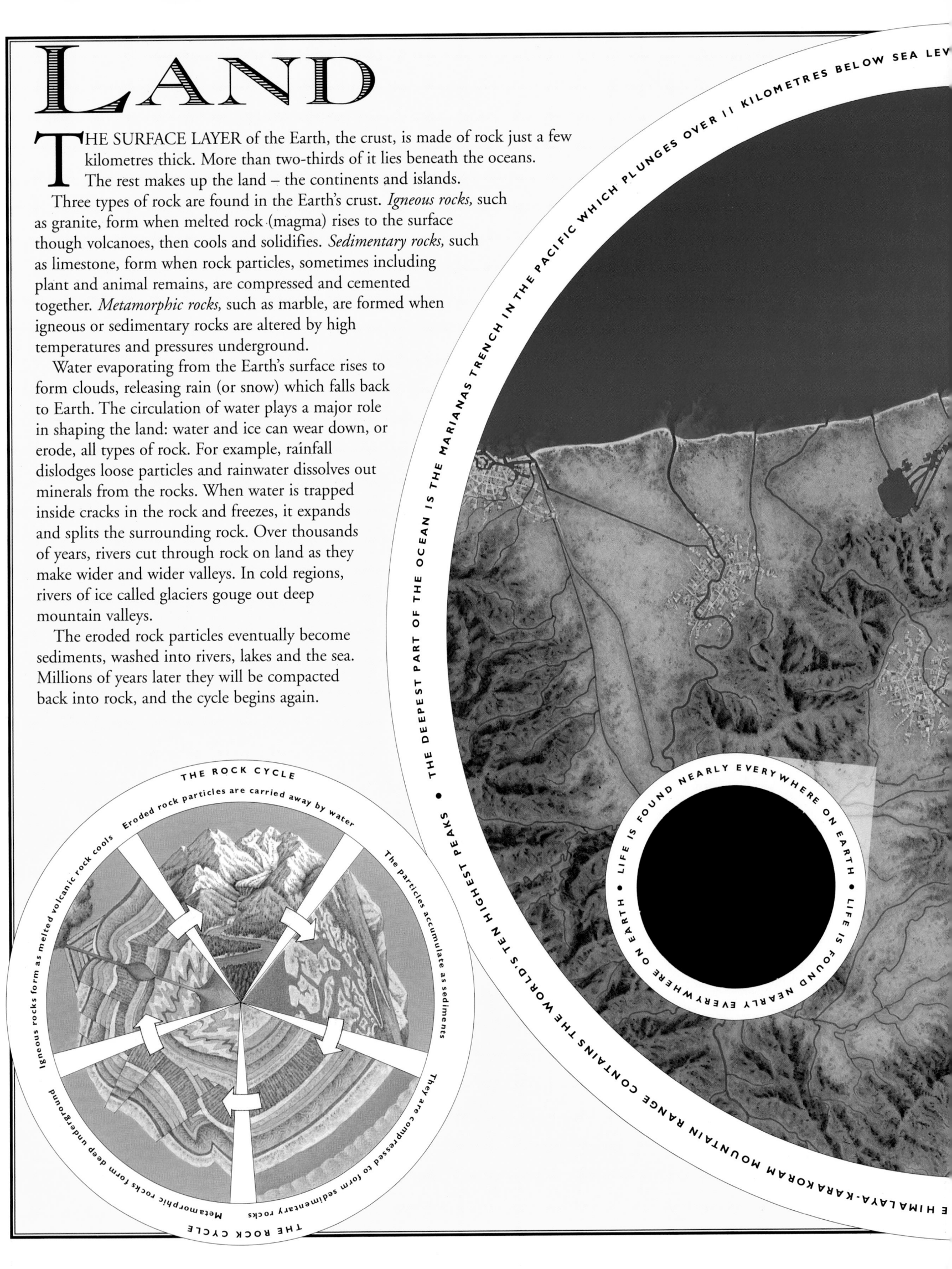

LAND

THE SURFACE LAYER of the Earth, the crust, is made of rock just a few kilometres thick. More than two-thirds of it lies beneath the oceans. The rest makes up the land – the continents and islands.

Three types of rock are found in the Earth's crust. *Igneous rocks,* such as granite, form when melted rock (magma) rises to the surface though volcanoes, then cools and solidifies. *Sedimentary rocks,* such as limestone, form when rock particles, sometimes including plant and animal remains, are compressed and cemented together. *Metamorphic rocks,* such as marble, are formed when igneous or sedimentary rocks are altered by high temperatures and pressures underground.

Water evaporating from the Earth's surface rises to form clouds, releasing rain (or snow) which falls back to Earth. The circulation of water plays a major role in shaping the land: water and ice can wear down, or erode, all types of rock. For example, rainfall dislodges loose particles and rainwater dissolves out minerals from the rocks. When water is trapped inside cracks in the rock and freezes, it expands and splits the surrounding rock. Over thousands of years, rivers cut through rock on land as they make wider and wider valleys. In cold regions, rivers of ice called glaciers gouge out deep mountain valleys.

The eroded rock particles eventually become sediments, washed into rivers, lakes and the sea. Millions of years later they will be compacted back into rock, and the cycle begins again.

THE ROCK CYCLE

Eroded rock particles are carried away by water

Igneous rocks form as melted volcanic rock cools

The particles accumulate as sediments

Metamorphic rocks form from deep underground

They are compressed to form sedimentary rocks

THE ROCK CYCLE

THE DEEPEST PART OF THE OCEAN IS THE MARIANAS TRENCH IN THE PACIFIC WHICH PLUNGES OVER 11 KILOMETRES BELOW SEA LEV

THE HIMALAYA-KARAKORAM MOUNTAIN RANGE CONTAINS THE WORLD'S TEN HIGHEST PEAKS

LIFE IS FOUND NEARLY EVERYWHERE ON EARTH • LIFE IS FOUND NEARLY EVERYWHERE ON EARTH • LIFE IS FOUND NEARLY EVERYWHERE ON EARTH

ENVIRONMENT

"AS I PLUMMET towards it, the scene below reveals more and more detailed shapes. Spread out like a patchwork quilt, there are fields of yellow, green and brown, all flat and smooth. Most are streaked with the lines of crops. Woods look like irregular, rougher-textured clumps of dark green and brown. The spindly lines of rivers I saw from a distance now show up as ribbons of deep blue wandering across the pattern. Occasional flecks of white show the rushing of water. The grey lines of roads – some straight, some with bends – criss-cross the scene. Here and there I can see the red roofs of houses and farms. All the while, birds flit past me in the air, emitting short, high-pitched cries."

DAYTIME SURFACE TEMPERATURES IN HOT DESERTS MAY REACH 90

DIFFERENT ENVIRONMENTS MAKE UP THE LANDSCAPE • DIFFERENT ENVIRONMENTS MAKE UP THE LANDSCAPE •

ANTARCTICA IS THE COLDEST PLACE ON EARTH: TEMPERATURES CAN BE AS LOW AS -88°C •

THE LARGEST HOT DESERT IS THE SAHARA • ...ND'S SURFACE

WORLD ENVIRONMENTS (1)

Desert

Tropical rainforest

Savannah (open grassland with trees)

Oceans

Coastal

Wetlands

WORLD ENVIRONMENTS (1)

ENVIRONMENT

THE ENVIRONMENT, our surroundings, includes the atmosphere, the continents, the oceans and the living things that inhabit them. Living organisms live in COMMUNITIES. These are collections of animals and plants which live in the same place and depend upon one another for their survival. The plants provide food for animals which, in turn, are eaten by other animals. Smaller ORGANISMS break down animal and plant waste (☞ SOIL), so releasing NUTRIENTS which plants can use.

The climate and physical landscape, including the nature of the underlying rock, determine the type of soil and the kinds of plants that can live in that area. The plant life, in turn, determines the types of animals that can thrive. Our world has many different climates and physical landscapes, so there are many different types of environment. Deserts, rainforests or grasslands, for example, each have their own distinctive communities.

In a woodland community, many kinds of insects, spiders and other small animals live in the trees or on the ground below. Various birds and mammals feed on these animals and they, in turn, may be preyed upon by other animals, such as birds of prey.

Human activities such as farming, city-building and industrial manufacturing have drastically altered the natural environment. In many parts of the world, the appearance of the countryside and the kinds of animals and plants that live there are the result of human activities.

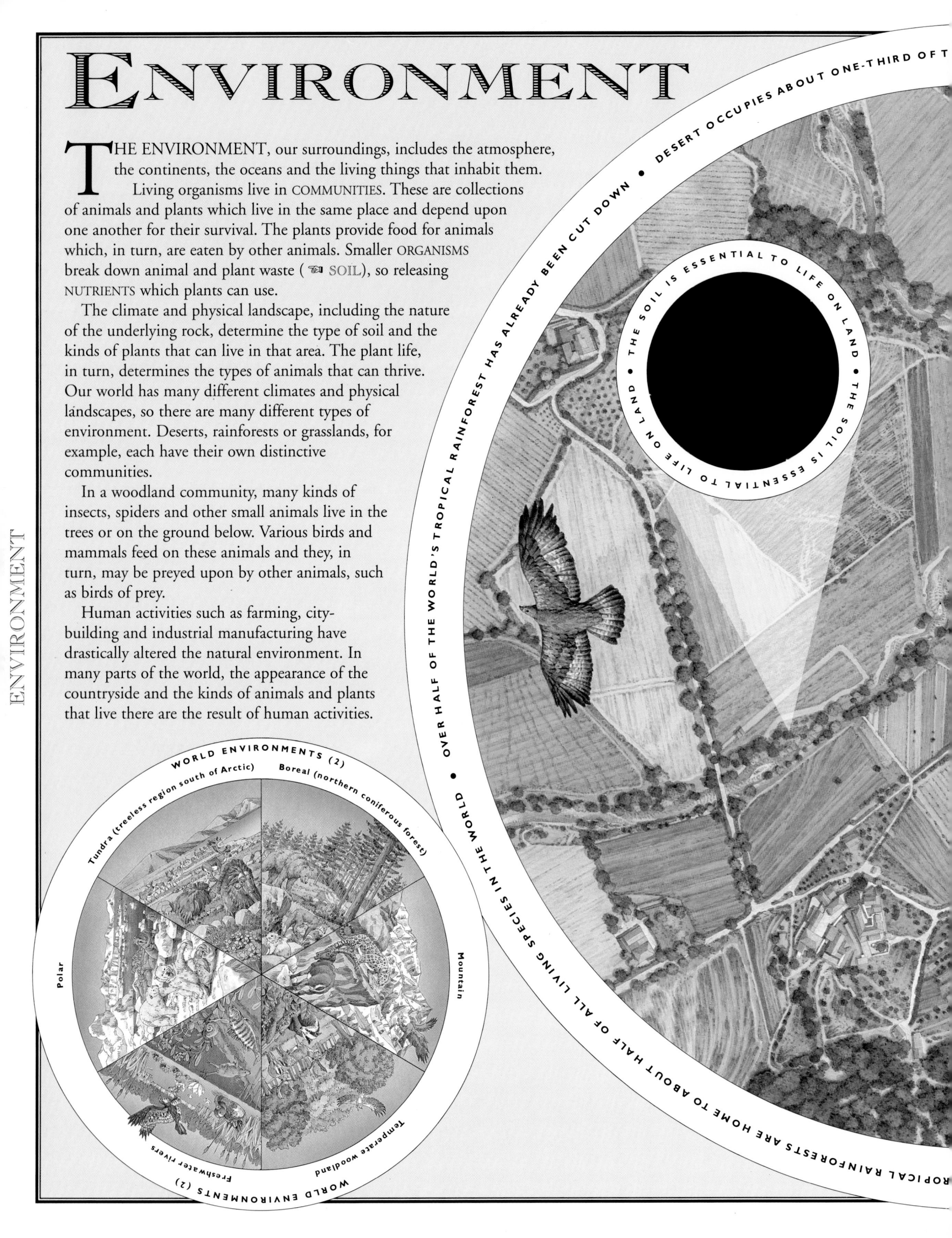

DESERT OCCUPIES ABOUT ONE-THIRD OF T

THE SOIL IS ESSENTIAL TO LIFE ON LAND • THE SOIL IS ESSENTIAL TO LIFE ON LAND

OVER HALF OF THE WORLD'S TROPICAL RAINFOREST HAS ALREADY BEEN CUT DOWN

TROPICAL RAINFORESTS ARE HOME TO ABOUT HALF OF ALL LIVING SPECIES IN THE WORLD

WORLD ENVIRONMENTS (2)

Tundra (treeless region south of Arctic)

Boreal (northern coniferous forest)

Mountain

Freshwater rivers

Temperate woodland

Polar

WORLD ENVIRONMENTS (2)

SOIL

> "SOFT, DARK BOULDERS press in on all sides. They are warm and damp, almost comforting. Against my cheek I can feel...things, millions of tiny, invisible things writhing and sliding. The air is heavy with an overpowering, sweet, woody scent. A giant, white finger – it must be a plant root – brushes against my face. Suddenly, the boulders start to shake and squash against me. There's a rumbling sound...getting louder and louder. The boulders are forced apart and a huge, wet, spongy wall of muscle shoves me backwards. It slithers over me, a seemingly endless, slippery steam-roller. A moment later, I hear eerie squeaks and scuttling sounds. I lift my head, and find myself face to face with great pincer-like jaws..."

LIVING IN ONE SQUARE KILOMETRE OF SOIL WILL BE AROUND 2

A PLANT'S FOOD IS MADE IN ITS LEAVES BY PHOTOSYNTHESIS • A MILLION PROTOZOANS (SINGLE-CELLED ORGANISMS) • OVER HALF A

SOIL IS A VITAL PART OF ALL LAND ENVIRONMENTS • SOIL IS A VITAL PART OF ALL LAND ENVIRONMENTS •

MAY CONTAIN OVER HALF A MILLION

ONE HEAPED TEASPOONFUL OF DAMP SOIL MAY CONTAIN

A PLANT'S FOOD IS MADE IN ITS LEAVES BY PHOTOSYNTHESIS

1 Carbon dioxide (CO2) is taken in from the air 2 Water is taken up from the soil 3 Sunlight provides energy 4 Sugars are made in the leaves from a reaction between CO2 and water 5 This food is transported to all parts of the plant

SOIL

SOIL IS A MIXTURE of tiny rock particles and humus – plant material that is in the process of decaying. Between the particles are large air spaces. These are important because they allow water to drain through the soil. They also allow oxygen to reach both the plant roots and the ORGANISMS (living things) that inhabit the soil.

All life on land depends on soil. Plants use it to anchor their roots. They take up water and minerals from the soil and transport them via the stem to the leaves where food is made by a process called PHOTOSYNTHESIS – a chemical reaction using sunlight. Most land animals feed on organisms that grow or live in the soil, either directly, or when they eat other animals that do so.

A handful of soil may not look very exciting. But it is like a giant factory where a mass of tiny organisms, most of which are too tiny to see with the naked eye, are working away recycling the remains of dead animals and plants into NUTRIENTS. These are in turn taken up by the roots of living plants. The tiniest of the "workers" are called BACTERIA. That handful of soil will contain over *10 billion* of them!

Microscopic organisms made of only one cell, called *protozoans,* feed on bacteria, while they are themselves eaten by larger animals such as worms. Earthworms also have a vital role to play tunnelling through the soil, letting air in, helping water drain through and mixing the different soil layers. Insects, spiders and centipedes hunt in the soil, and larger animals like moles and voles make their burrows there.

IT TAKES ABOUT 10,000 YEARS FOR A MATURE SOIL TO FORM OVER UNDERLYING ROC

SEVERAL TONNES OF SOIL EACH YEAR • MANY TINY FORMS OF LIFE ARE FOUND IN SOIL • MANY TINY FORMS OF LIFE ARE FOUND IN SOIL • MANY TINY FORMS OF LIFE ARE FOUND IN SOIL • EARTHWORMS IN A SMALL FIELD WILL SWALLOW

SPIDERS • LLION

VITAL CYCLES

Animals feed on plants growing in the soil

Nutrients are released and taken up by plants

Waste, dead animals and plants decay

Tiny organisms turn remains into nutrients

VITAL CYCLES

ANIMAL

" *ABOVE THE JAWS* are two giant, bulbous eyes. I can't tell whether the creature has seen me: there are no irises or pupils in its eyes, only a gauze-like texture covering them. Below the jaws, smaller mouthparts twitch menacingly, slavering for a meal. Two long, rod-like antennae project forward from its head just in front of its eyes. They wave around in what seems a random fashion, constantly probing the ground ahead of it. Then there is a cracking sound as its legs push into the soil like the arms of a mechanical excavator. The creature edges forward, its head moving from side to side. Now I can see its back – smooth, glossy and vivid green with bright yellow spots regularly arranged in a pattern. It looks like a robot in medieval armour!* "

THERE ARE PROBABLY ONE MILLION TIMES MORE INSECTS ON THE PLANET THAN THERE ARE HUMAN BEINGS • MANY SMALL ANIMALS ARE FOUND IN THE SOIL • MANY SMALL ANIMALS ARE FOUND IN THE SOIL • SEVERAL THOUSAND NEW KINDS OF INSECT ARE DISCOVERED EACH YEAR •

LIFE CYCLE OF THE FIELD TIGER BEETLE

Adults mate to produce offspring

An adult emerges from the pupa in spring

Eggs are laid singly in the soil

A larva hatches from the egg and grows

The mature larva changes into a pupa

LIFE CYCLE OF THE FIELD TIGER BEETLE

ANIMAL

OVER TWO MILLION KINDS of animal live on Planet Earth. They range in size from microscopic forms to giants such as the blue whale, which can weigh 160 tonnes or so. About half of all animals are insects – small, land-living creatures coated in a smooth, shiny, armour-like skeleton. The body of an insect is always divided into three parts: the head, the middle *(thorax)* and the hind region *(abdomen)*. An insect has six legs and, usually, wings for flight. Beetles are the most abundant kind of insect.

One key difference between animals and plants is the way they feed. Most plants take in simple chemicals from the soil and air and use sunlight energy to convert these into food substances (☞ SOIL). Animals, on the other hand, obtain their food by eating plants or other animals. Once swallowed, their food is broken down (digested) and then distributed around the body by a transport system, usually a system of tubes containing blood pumped by a beating heart. The food substances are either chemically altered and used to construct body parts, or broken down – with the help of oxygen the animal has breathed in – to release energy. Waste products are removed (excreted) from the animal's body.

An animal's eyes, ears and other sense organs detect features of its surroundings and help the animal find its food. A nervous system delivers information from the sense organs to the brain, which then sends messages to the muscles to control body movement.

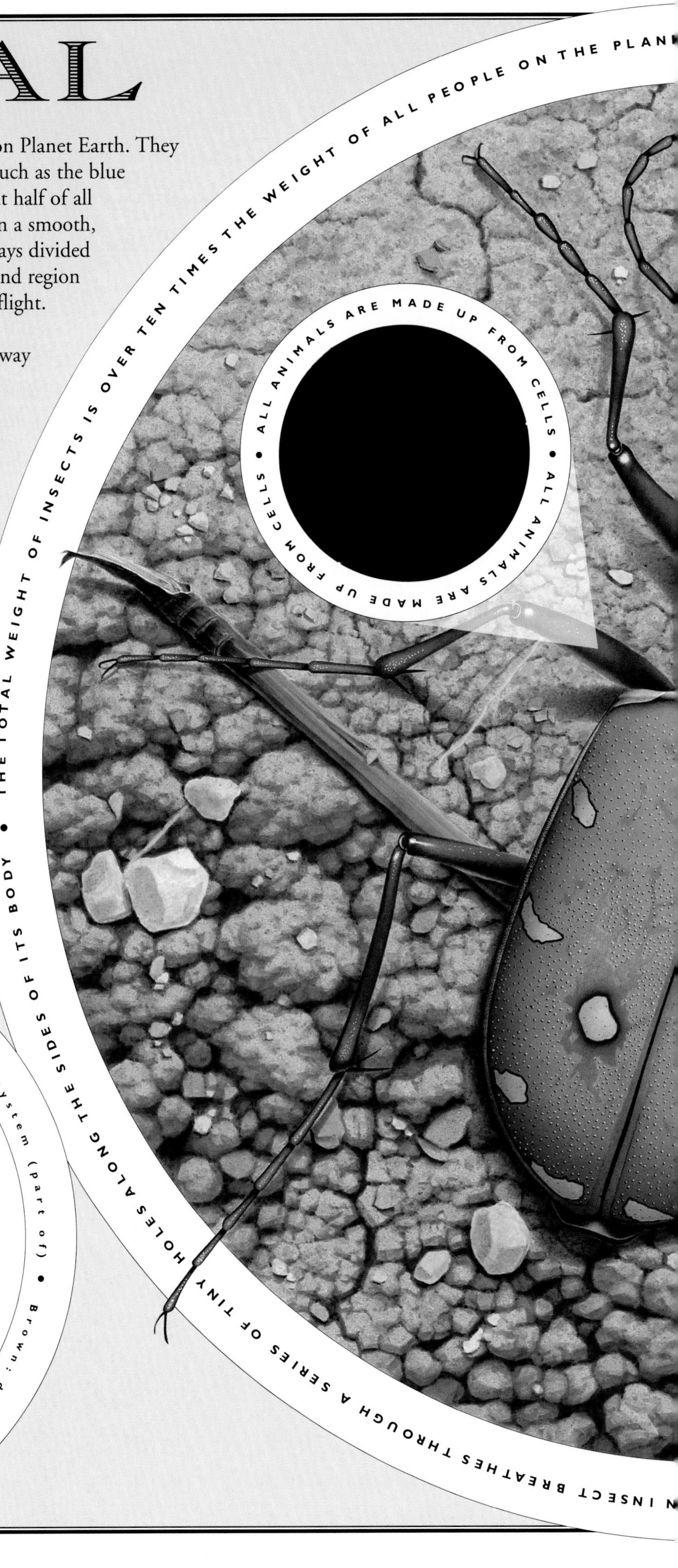

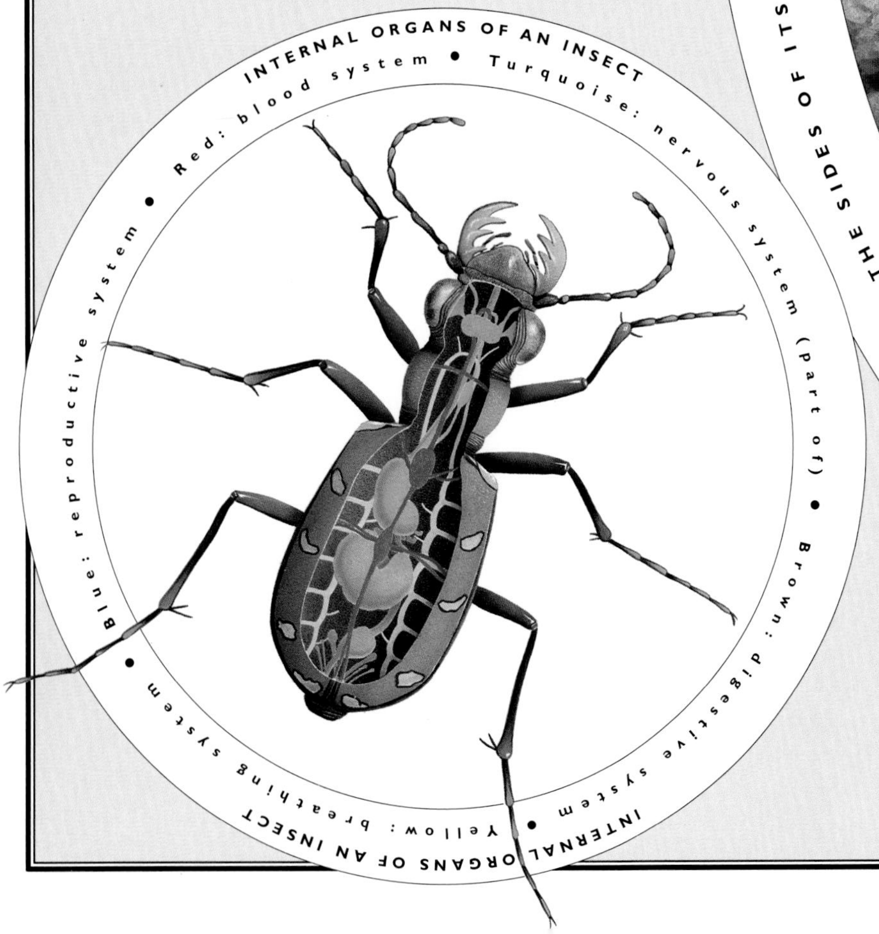

THE TOTAL WEIGHT OF INSECTS IS OVER TEN TIMES THE WEIGHT OF ALL PEOPLE ON THE PLAN[ET]

ALL ANIMALS ARE MADE UP FROM CELLS • ALL ANIMALS ARE MADE UP FROM CELLS •

AN INSECT BREATHES THROUGH A SERIES OF TINY HOLES ALONG THE SIDES OF ITS BODY •

INTERNAL ORGANS OF AN INSECT • Red: blood system • Turquoise: nervous system (part of) • Brown: digestive system • Yellow: breathing system • INTERNAL ORGANS OF AN INSECT • Blue: reproductive system •

CELL

"*I PLUNGE* through a hard, almost impenetrable barrier. Now I'm floating in what feels like thick soup. Disc-shaped objects waft past me like giant rugs, their surfaces blistering and popping to release small, glutinous spheres. Giant globules wobble by. One devours a small sphere that drifts too close. This soup seems to be "alive" with tiny things I cannot see. A huge, cigar-shaped creation cruises along somewhere above my head. Then, rearing up ahead of me, a vast, smooth wall. But, as I near it, as if it knew I was there, the mouth of a tunnel opens up ahead. I swim through. Coming the other way are what seems like thousands of squirming, wriggling eels, all far too tiny to see.*"

▶ An array of approximately rectangular cells are packed together to make up an insect's outer body layer

THE SMALLEST CELLS BELONG TO BACTERIA, SIMPLE SINGLE-CELLED ORGANI

THE SMALLEST CELLS IN THE HUMAN BODY; IT IS ABOUT THE SIZE OF A FULL STOP •

THE EGG CELL IS ONE OF THE LARGEST CELLS IN THE HUMAN BODY; • THE EGG CELL IS ONE OF THE LARGEST

CELLS ARE THE BUILDING BLOCKS OF LIFE • CELLS ARE THE BUILDING BLOCKS OF LIFE • CELLS ARE THE BUILDING BLOCKS OF LIFE • CELLS

LION CELLS IN THE HUMAN BODY •

AN ORGANISM GROWS BY CELL DIVISION

▲ The cell divides with identical DNA contained in each cell 1 Chromosomes, containing DNA, are located in the nucleus 2 Each chromosome splits in two. 3 Two cell nuclei are formed

① ② ③ ④

AN ORGANISM GROWS BY CELL DIVISION

CELL

MOST PLANTS AND ANIMALS contain millions, sometimes even billions of CELLS. Each cell is microscopic in size, but they combine to form all body parts. The cells are the building blocks of the body, in the same way that bricks fit together to make buildings. Cells, however, come in many different shapes and sizes.

Every cell is surrounded by a thin, sieve-like barrier, a cell membrane. This controls which substances enter or leave the cell. Inside the membrane, there is a mass of jelly with various parts suspended in it. The cell is like a factory where some chemicals are broken down and others built up. Sausage-shaped structures called *mitochondria* (shown in red in this illustration) provide the "power". Other structures form mazes of tubes through which chemicals are transported around the cell. Still others make substances which are released into the surroundings. The cells in this illustration, for example, make the chemical *chitin* which forms part of the insect's tough outer coat.

The nucleus, the region in the centre (shown here as grey), is like the computer program which runs the cell. It contains CHROMOSOMES, into which DNA is tightly wound. Most animals and plants begin life as a single, fertilized egg cell. For the ORGANISM to grow, the cell has to divide and divide again many times over. The chromosomes split in two each time, so, as the organism grows, its cells contain identical DNA.

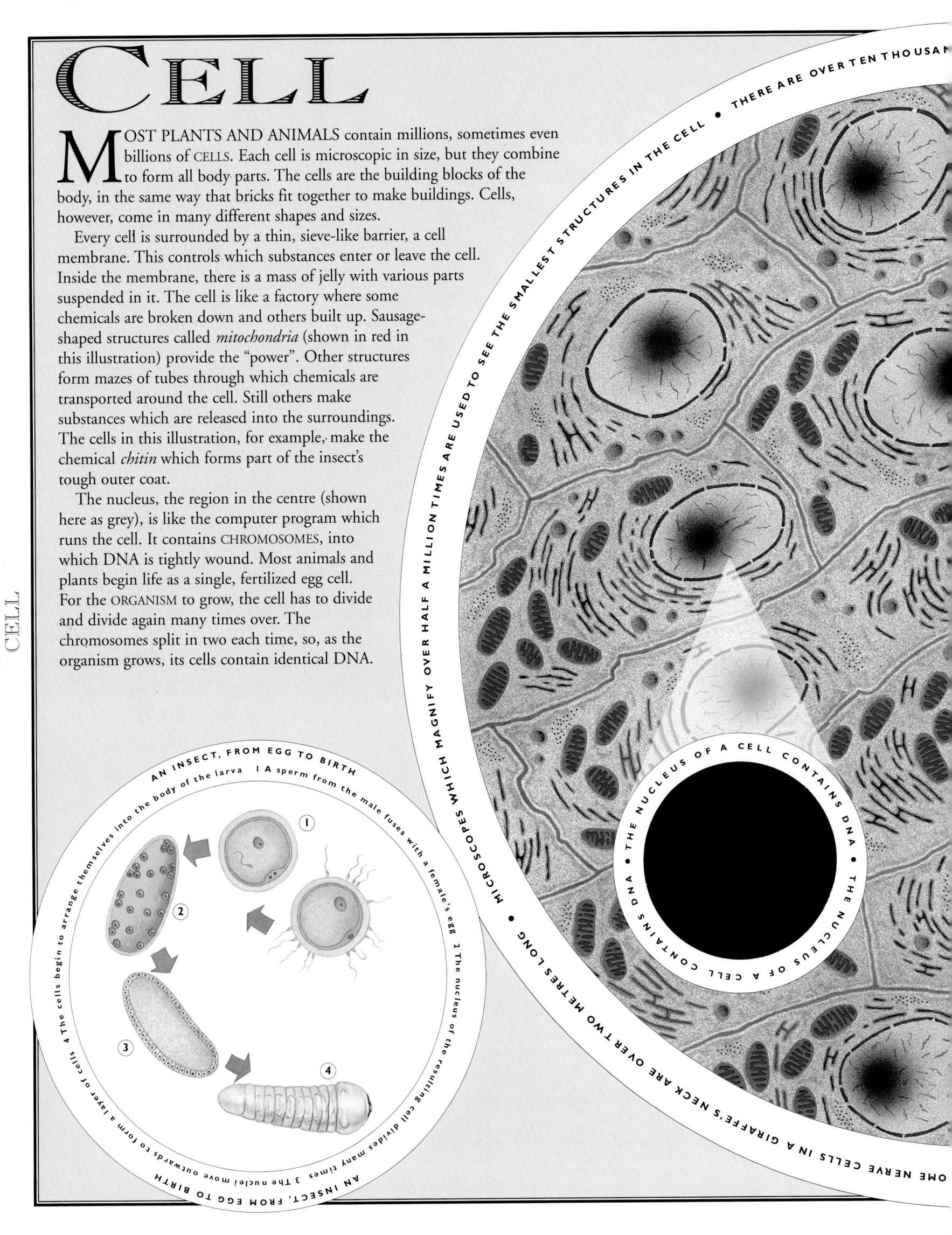

THERE ARE OVER TEN THOUSAND OF THE SMALLEST STRUCTURES IN THE CELL

MICROSCOPES WHICH MAGNIFY OVER HALF A MILLION TIMES ARE USED TO SEE THE SMALLEST STRUCTURES IN THE CELL

THE NUCLEUS OF A CELL CONTAINS DNA • THE NUCLEUS OF A CELL CONTAINS DNA

SOME NERVE CELLS IN A GIRAFFE'S NECK ARE OVER TWO METRES LONG

AN INSECT, FROM EGG TO BIRTH

1 A sperm from the male fuses with a female's egg 2 The nucleus of the resulting cell divides many times 3 The nuclei move outwards to form a layer of cells 4 The cells begin to arrange themselves into the body of the larva

AN INSECT, FROM EGG TO BIRTH

① ② ③ ④

DNA

"*SPREAD BEFORE ME is a huge expanse of what looks like tangled rope. Close to, I can see that it is made up of two strands twisted around each other. The two strands are knitted together by innumerable linking strands. The rope is a hive of activity. Large blobs drift up to the edge of it, seem to attach themselves, and then float off again. I see parts of the rope unravelling themselves, their two strands unwinding and drifting apart. Then there is a flurry of activity around one of the unwound strands. One large blob moves in, slides along that strand, and leaves behind a new strand lying alongside it. The new strand now breaks away and the rope then winds itself up again.*"

▶ Long, spiral strands of DNA are found inside a cell's nucleus

THERE IS ENOUGH DNA IN • DNA IS FOUND IN THE NUCLEUS OF A CELL • A HUMAN CELL HAS ABOUT TWO METRES • DNA IS FOUND IN THE NUCLEUS OF A CELL • DNA IS FOUND IN THE NUCLEUS OF A CELL • EACH CELL OF A FRUITFLY CONTAINS ABOUT 10 CENTIMETRES OF DNA • A DNA MOLECULE MAY CONTAIN OVER 1000 MILLION ATOMS

HOW DNA IS FOLDED UP INTO CHROMOSOMES

▶ Chromatin fibres consist of coils of DNA strands wrapped around protein molecules

▼ DNA consists of two spirals linked by chemical bridges

Chromosomes are made up of loops of chromatin fibres

▼ HOW DNA IS FOLDED UP INTO CHROMOSOMES

DNA

DNA (short for **D**eoxyribo**N**ucleic **A**cid) is a giant MOLECULE found in the nucleus of CELLS. Enormously long and complex, it contains the instructions for building and maintaining the cell. Since most cells in the body of a plant or animal contain identical DNA, this chemical contains the instructions for building the entire bodies of plants and animals.

The DNA molecule is like a long, spiral ladder, sometimes called a double helix. The two twisted "uprights" of the ladder are linked together by chemical bridges which form the "rungs". These chemical bridges are of four kinds. The exact order in which they appear on the ladder is like a code.

A GENE is a short section of DNA. The code sequences in genes carry instructions for making PROTEINS, substances which provide the material for building cells. There are thousands of different proteins in cells and each carries out a particular job. For instructions to be issued, part of the DNA molecule must unwind to expose the chemical code on its rungs. The code is copied and the copy leaves the nucleus. The cell is then instructed to make a particular protein.

There are several lengths of DNA inside a cell's nucleus. (Interestingly, only one per cent of the DNA in a human cell is used to control its activities. The rest is redundant.) Each length is combined with other substances to form a CHROMOSOME. DNA is folded up into the chromosome very tightly indeed.

DNA MAKES COPIES OF ITSELF

1 Each strand with its sequence of rungs provides instructions for the creation of new DNA

2 DNA "unzips" itself

3 A new strand is made by copying the sequence of rungs

A CHROMOSOME MAY BE 10,000 TIMES SHORTER THAN THE LENGTH OF DNA IT CONTAI[NS] • DNA IS MADE UP FROM SMALLER MOLECULES • DNA IS MADE UP FROM SMALLER MOLECULES • GENES, HUMANS 100,000 GENES • A CHROMOSOME MAY BE 10,000 TIMES • [H]UMAN TO GO AROUND THE EARTH 700,000 TIMES • FRUITFLIES HAVE AROUND 5,000 GENES

DNA

MOLECULE

"

THE WINDING STRANDS are made of clusters of what look like beads. There are thousands of them, some arranged in neat rings, others in straggly chains. But there is definite order: the patterns seem to repeat themselves. All the beads wobble and shake as though they are alive. Sometimes they twist and writhe – particularly when other drifting clusters of beads come by. In fact, the whole scene around me is alive with tiny beads zipping to and fro, moving much faster than those held in the clutches of the giant chains. I fall towards one of the beads. As it fills my entire field of vision, I realise the surface of the bead is not solid at all...

"

▶ A substance like **DNA**, a large molecule, is made up of connected "beads" called atoms

GAS (e.g. STEAM)

Molecules are fast-moving and widely separated

SOLID (e.g. ICE) Molecules are packed together in a regular arrangement

LIQUID (e.g. WATER) Molecules are slow-moving and quite close together

MANY OF THE MOLECULES IN LIVING THINGS DO NOT EXIST AT ALL IN THE NON-LIVING WORLD • MANY OF THE MOLECULES IN THE HUMAN BODY • THERE ARE AT LEAST 10,000 DIFFERENT KINDS OF MOLECULE IN THE HUMAN BODY • DNA IS A CARBON-BASED MOLECULE • DNA IS A CARBON-BASED MOLECULE • ATLANTIC OCEAN • THERE ARE AT LEAST 10,000 DIFFERENT KINDS OF MOLECULE

MOLECULE

W HEN ATOMS ARE JOINED together by strong chemical bonds (☞ ATOM) they form MOLECULES. In some cases, a molecule is formed from two or more atoms of the same type. For example, a molecule of oxygen gas (written in chemical shorthand as O_2) contains two atoms of oxygen. There are a great many examples of molecules containing two or more atoms of different kinds. A molecule of water (H_2O), for instance, contains two hydrogen atoms and one oxygen atom. A molecule of carbon dioxide (CO_2) contains one carbon atom and two oxygen atoms.

Living things contain tens of thousands of different molecules of various shapes and sizes. The most abundant molecule in living things, and one of the simplest, is water. The largest is *deoxyribonucleic acid* (DNA for short). Many of the larger and more important molecules in living things contain the element carbon.

A giant molecule like DNA is formed by combining together smaller molecules. In DNA, these molecules join together to form two very long chains.

The common chemical ELEMENTS in the bodies of animals and plants are all present in the air or the rocks which make up the Earth's crust (☞ LAND). What is special is the way these elements are combined as molecules inside living things. These molecules work together to repair and maintain all working parts of a living thing, and to produce offspring in the same form.

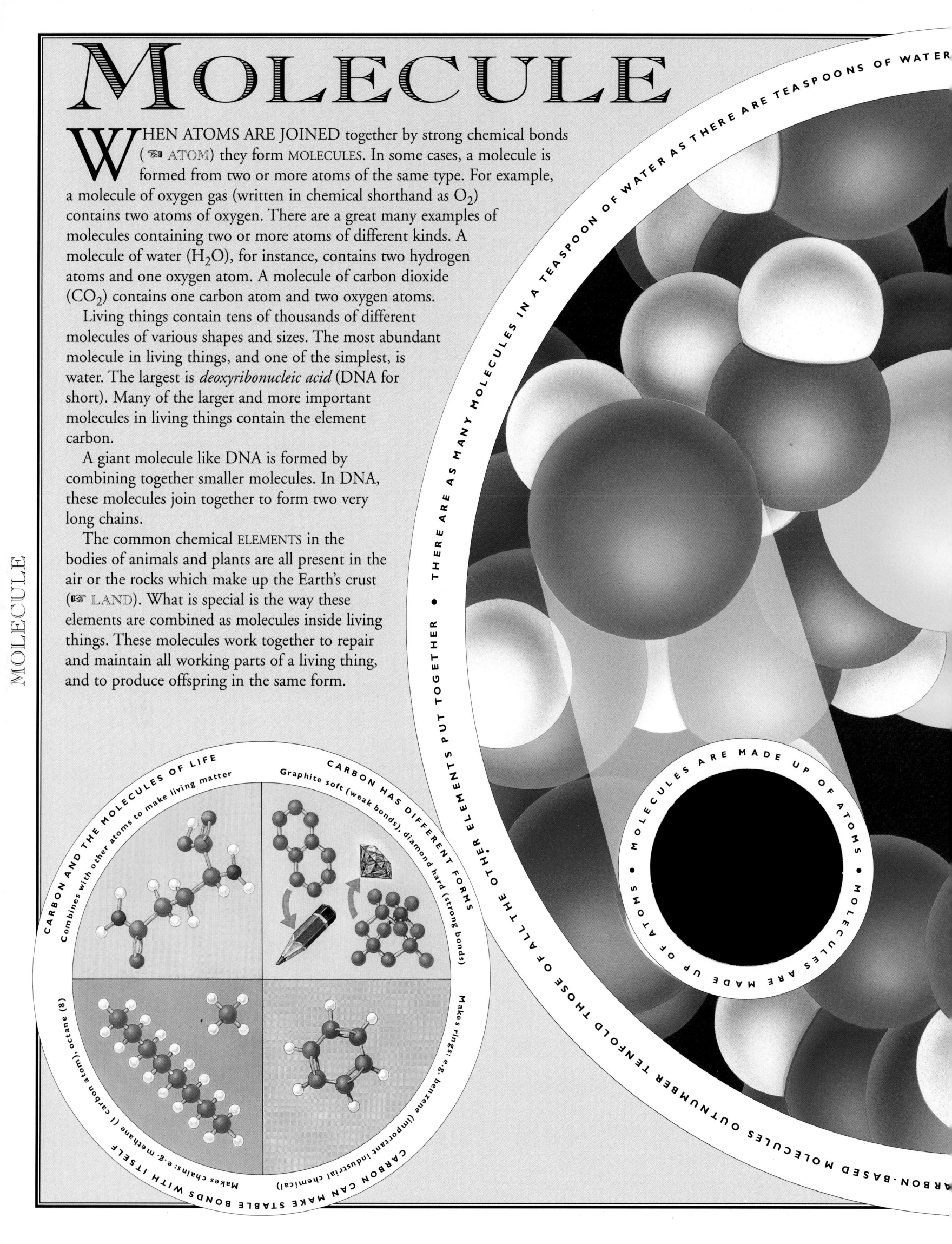

THERE ARE AS MANY MOLECULES IN A TEASPOON OF WATER AS THERE ARE TEASPOONS OF WATER

MOLECULES ARE MADE UP OF ATOMS • MOLECULES ARE MADE UP OF ATOMS • MOLECULES ARE MADE UP OF ATOMS

IN ALL THE OTHER ELEMENTS PUT TOGETHER • CARBON-BASED MOLECULES OUTNUMBER TENFOLD THOSE OF ALL THE OTHER ELEMENTS PUT TOGETHER

CARBON AND THE MOLECULES OF LIFE
Combines with other atoms to make living matter

CARBON HAS DIFFERENT FORMS
Graphite soft (weak bonds), diamond hard (strong bonds)

Makes rings: e.g. benzene (important industrial chemical)

Makes chains: e.g. methane (1 carbon atom), octane (8)

CARBON CAN MAKE STABLE BONDS WITH ITSELF

ATOM

" *I AM FALLING, through nothing. It's like being in space again. Points of light fizz past me, tiny balls of electricity crackling as they go. I count six in all. Comets? A seventh dot of light remains motionless in the distance, twinkling like a star. I start to feel that I am not only falling, I am actually being dragged towards this light. Some sort of giant magnet? Faster and faster I go: whatever it is, I can't resist its pull. The crackle of electricity is intense. The dot has ballooned into a swirling sphere of light. Its pull is too much to bear...the force is beginning to crush me. In a fraction of a second, the globe fills my entire vision. My senses explode as I plunge straight into it...* "

▶ Inside a carbon atom, electrons orbit the nucleus, a cluster of protons and neutrons

IF A NUCLEUS WAS A GOLF BALL IN THE CENTRE OF A STADIUM, THE EDGE OF THE ATOM

ATOMS BOND TOGETHER TO FORM MOLECULES • ATOMS BOND TOGETHER TO FORM MOLECULES

100,000 TIMES SMALLER THAN THE WHOLE ATOM • THE NUCLEUS IS

HYDROGEN ATOM IS ABOUT ONE TEN MILLIONTH OF A MILLIMETRE ACROSS

ELEMENTS HAVE DIFFERENT NUMBERS OF ELECTRONS AND PROTONS IN THEIR ATOMS

The sun is mostly made of hydrogen

Neon is used to make electric lights

Lead is used to make shot gun pellets

Sulphur is found in egg yolks

Silver is used to make jewellery

Calcium is found in chalk, milk and bones

ELEMENTS HAVE DIFFERENT NUMBERS OF ELECTRONS AND PROTONS IN THEIR ATOMS

BAR

ATOM

ALL SUBSTANCES are composed from 92 naturally occurring ELEMENTS and an ATOM is the smallest part of an element that can exist. Atoms are so small that the full-stop at the end of this sentence contains more than *one billion* of them.

Tiny as it is, an atom is almost entirely made up of empty space. The rest consists of protons, neutrons and ELECTRONS. Protons and neutrons are found clustered together in a minute, extremely dense nucleus at the very centre of the atom. Little bundles of energy called electrons whizz around this nucleus at the speed of light. It is the presence of electrons that make the atom behave like a solid, in the same way that a fan blade spinning rapidly looks and behaves as if it were solid.

In an atom there are the same number of electrons as there are protons. Both have electrical charges: electrons negative, protons positive. Unlike charges attract, and so the atom is held together. Each of the 92 elements has a different number of electrons and protons in their atoms.

Electrons bond one atom to another to make MOLECULES. When two atoms share a pair of electrons this forms a *covalent bond*. When an electron leaves one atom and enters another, the two atoms become IONS held together by an *ionic bond*. Other types of bond include *metallic bonds*, in which the outer electrons float around in a common pool, and *hydrogen bonds* found between water molecules, in which positively charged hydrogen atoms are attracted to negatively charged oxygen atoms.

THE GREEK PHILOSOPHER DEMOCRITUS (460–400 BC) WAS THE FIRST TO SUGGEST THAT MATTER WAS MADE UP OF TINY PARTICLES • PROTONS AND NEUTRONS ARE MADE UP OF PARTICLES • PROTONS AND NEUTRONS ARE MADE UP OF PARTICLES

PROTONS ARE ABOUT 2,000 TIMES HEAVIER THAN ELECTRONS • ... WOULD BE THE STADIUM'S OUTER WALL

ATOMS BOND IN DIFFERENT WAYS

A hydrogen bond between water molecules

An ionic bond between sodium and chlorine ions

In a metallic bond outer electrons move around freely

Covalent bond between hydrogen and oxygen atoms (water)

ATOMS BOND IN DIFFERENT WAYS

PARTICLE

"*I FEEL LIKE a rubber band stretched to the limit – and someone has just let me go. I snap back into shape. All around me rages a high-speed buzz of activity. Large, fuzzy objects appear and disappear so quickly that, before I can focus on them, they're gone. There seem to be hundreds of them winking and flashing at me. But who can tell? Perhaps it's only one, dancing around, madly. The force that is holding me here is just enormous. Every time I try to make a move, I feel that stretched rubber band holding me in its grip. The harder I try, the stronger the force seems to be. I'm not sure whether I am ever going to escape from here...*"

▶ The proton (shown here in red) and neutron (black) particles at the very centre of an atom contain quarks (represented by blue and white balls) and gluons (gold balls)

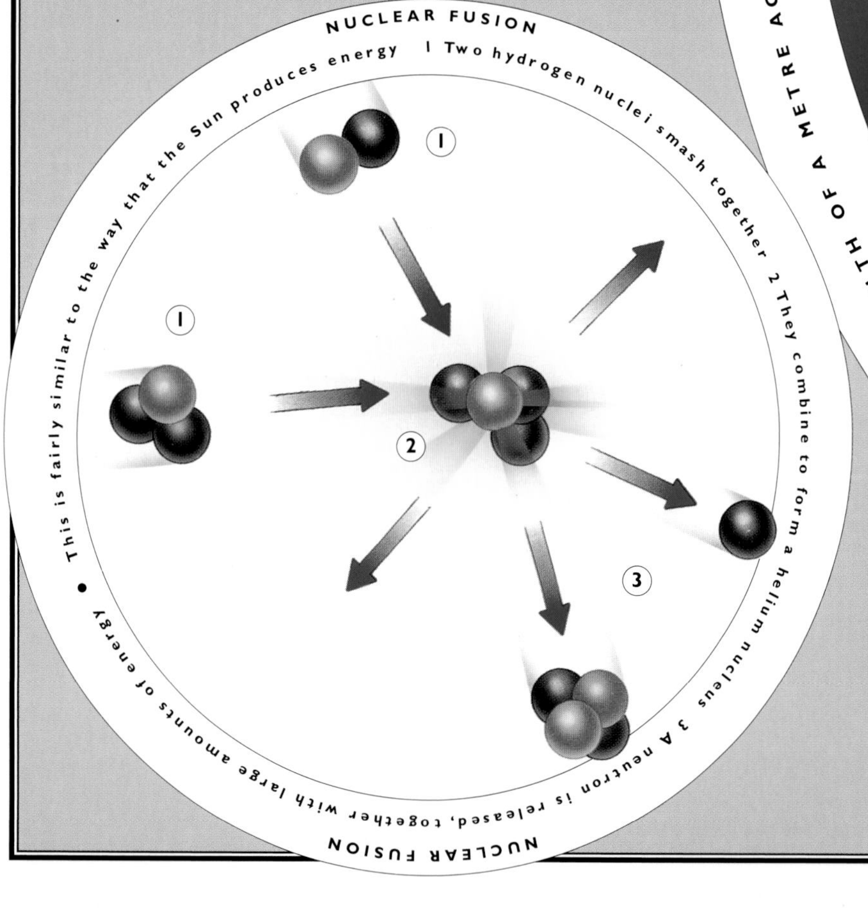

MORE THAN 200 KINDS OF SUB-ATOMIC PARTICLES HAVE NOW BEEN DISCOVERED • THE NAME QUA

A BILLION-BILLIONTH OF A METRE ACROSS

ATOMS ARE MADE UP OF PARTICLES • ATOMS ARE MADE UP OF PARTICLES • ATOMS ARE MADE UP OF PARTICLES

THE NUCLEUS OF A HYDROGEN ATOM IS ABOUT A MILLION

NUCLEAR FUSION

This is fairly similar to the way that the Sun produces energy   1 Two hydrogen nuclei smash together   2 They combine to form a helium nucleus   3 A neutron is released, together with large amounts of energy

NUCLEAR FUSION

① 1

② 2

③ 3

PARTICLE

THE ATOM is the smallest part of a substance. But an atom is not the smallest thing there is. Inside an atom are even smaller, SUB-ATOMIC PARTICLES. Most of these are crammed into the tiny nucleus at the centre of the atom (the other sub-atomic particles are ELECTRONS ☞ ATOM). Particles with a positive electrical charge, called *protons,* and neutral particles, called *neutrons,* jostle for space inside the atom's minute nucleus.

A very powerful force keeps these two kinds of particles together. It is called the *strong nuclear force* and operates at the tiny distances found within the nucleus.

Incredibly, protons and neutrons are themselves formed from still smaller particles, called *quarks.* Protons and neutrons both contain three quarks, but they contain a different balance of two kinds of quark, known as "up" or "down". Neutrons contain one up quark and two down quarks, while protons contain two up quarks and one down quark. Protons can readily change into neutrons, and vice versa, by changing one of their quarks.

The strong nuclear force of the nucleus is carried by other sub-atomic particles, called *gluons,* which lie among the quarks. When nuclei collide and join together *(nuclear fusion),* as happens in the Sun (☞ SOLAR SYSTEM), the strong nuclear force is released as massive amounts of energy. Nuclear energy can also be released when atomic nuclei are split apart. This process is called *nuclear fission:* it is used in nuclear power stations.

PHYSICISTS DISTINGUISH BETWEEN THE 18 KINDS OF QUARK BY THEIR DIFFERENT "COLOURS" AND "FLAVOURS" • QUARK IS A NONSENSE WORD USED BY THE AMERICAN PHYSICIST MURRAY GELL-MANN

NUCLEAR FISSION

A The released neutrons blast into other uranium atomic nuclei | A neutron smashes into nucleus of a uranium atom 2 Nucleus splits in two 3 Neutrons are released, together with large amounts of energy

NUCLEAR FISSION

THE INCREDIBLE JOURNEY TO THE EDGE OF THE UNIVERSE

TAKE ANY OBJECT: a chair, an insect, or even just the air around us. You may already know that all these are made up of minute particles called atoms. But did you know that atoms themselves are also made up of particles? They are so small that scientists cannot see them, even through the most powerful of microscopes. But they are the tiny building blocks from which the entire Universe is made.

If particles come together, they make atoms. If atoms join up, molecules are produced. The organs essential to life are made of molecules. Animals, plants, and other forms of life share the planet Earth, itself one of the Sun's family of planets. And the Sun is one star in the Milky Way Galaxy – just one galaxy in billions that make up the Universe.

This book takes you on a journey of exploration through the Universe...